Desserts in a Jar: The Best 50 Mason Jar Desserts That Are Quick and Easy to Make

Click Here To Receive Free Kindle Books To Your Email Daily

Promo Kindle
Knowledge is better when it's free

www.PromoKindle.com

All rights Reserved. No part of this publication or the information in it may be quoted from or reproduced in any form by means such as printing, scanning, photocopying or otherwise without prior written permission of the copyright holder.

Disclaimer and Terms of Use: Effort has been made to ensure that the information in this book is accurate and complete, however, the author and the publisher do not warrant the accuracy of the information, text and graphics contained within the book due to the rapidly changing nature of science, research, known and unknown facts and internet. The Author and the publisher do not hold any responsibility for errors, omissions or contrary interpretation of the subject matter herein. This book is presented solely for motivational and informational purposes only.

Table of Contents

Caramel brownie 7

S'mores in Mason jar 9

Raspberry cheesecake in jar 11

Cherry pie in jar 12

Lazy cheesecake with lemon and strawberries 14

Berry cream pie 16

Peach cobbler in jar 18

Banana split in jar 20

Raspberry-Mascarpone cream dessert 21

Oreo cookie butter 23

Cherry crisp in jar 24

Chocolate cheesecake 26

Grasshopper pies 28

Maple-pecan pie 30

Monkey bread in jar 32

Strawberry shortcake 34

Whiskey-chocolate cake 36

Hot chocolate cupcakes 37

No-bake cheesecake 39

Peanut butter-chocolate cupcakes 41

Carrot cake in jar 43

Blueberry pies 44

Pretzel-strawberry dessert 46

Apple custard pie 48

Eclairs in jar 50

Dark chocolate chips bread pudding 52

Banana pudding 54

Baked fudge 56

Italian caramel pudding 58

Pumpkin-coffee pie in jar 60

Coconut simple cake 62

Blackberry cream pie 64

Lemon raspberry mousse pie 66

Raisins and yogurt cake 68

Cherry-chocolate cake 70

Crème brulee with ginger 71

After Eight mini cakes 73

Ice cream pie 75

Butterscotch lava cake 77

Pumpkin panna cotta 79

Almond and orange cake 81

Butter pudding cakes 83

Baked chocolate mousse 85

Fast peanut butter and chocolate cake 87

Sweet potato cake in jar 89

Almond cake in jar 91

Mango float 93

Banana whipped cream and strawberries dessert 95

Butterscotch crème 97

Peanut butter pie 99

Caramel brownie

Serves: 6

Time: 20 minutes

Ingredients:

- 6 brownies, store bought
- 2 cups whipped cream
- ½ cup heavy cream
- ¼ cup chocolate pudding, store bought
- ½ stick butter
- 1 cup brown sugar
- ¼ cup chocolate chips
- 1 pinch salt

Directions:

1. Prepare the caramel sauce; melt butter in sauce pan; add sugar and stir until melted. Stir in pinch of salt and pour over heavy cream; whisk until all combined evenly. Place aside.
2. Cube brownies and divide them in the bottom of six wide mouth Mason jars; ladle a good layer prepared caramel sauce over brownies.
3. Top with layer of whipped cream, layer of chocolate pudding and layer of chocolate chips. Add one layer of cubed brownies, pour over caramel sauce and finish with whipped cream. Serve chilled.

S'mores in Mason jar

Serves: 6

Time: 20 minutes

Ingredients:

- 12oz. semi-sweet chocolate, chopped
- 1 stick butter, melted
- 1 ¼ cups graham crackers
- 1 tablespoon sugar
- 12oz. marshmallow fluff
- 1 cup heavy cream

Directions:

1. Place the graham crackers in food processor; pulse until ground.
2. Add in melted butter and sugar; pulse until combined.
3. Place the chopped chocolate in ceramic bowl. Heat the heavy cream, until almost simmering and pour over chocolate; stir to combine.
4. Divide graham cracker mixture between six wide mouth jars, pressing slightly to the bottom.
5. Divide chocolate over graham cracker crust and top with marshmallow fluff. Place the dessert under broiler and broil for 5 minutes.
6. Serve immediately.

Nutrition Facts

Serving Size 172 g

Amount Per Serving

Calories 750	Calories from Fat 339
	% Daily Value*
Total Fat 37.6g	58%
Saturated Fat 21.2g	106%
Trans Fat 0.0g	
Cholesterol 87mg	29%
Sodium 491mg	20%
Potassium 43mg	1%
Total Carbohydrates 101.5g	34%
Dietary Fiber 2.4g	9%
Sugars 59.7g	
Protein 3.7g	

Vitamin A 21%	•	Vitamin C 0%
Calcium 4%	•	Iron 9%

Nutrition Grade D

* Based on a 2000 calorie diet

Raspberry cheesecake in jar

Serves: 24 mini cakes

Time: 40 minutes

Ingredients:

- 2 cups graham crackers, ground
- 8 tablespoons butter, melted
- 1 teaspoon pure vanilla extract
- 32oz. cream cheese, room temperature
- 1 cup sour cream
- Zest of 1 lemon
- ¾ cup sugar
- 4 eggs
- 4 cups raspberries, fresh
- 1/3 cup raspberry jelly

Directions:

1. Preheat oven to 325F and spray mini jars with cooking oil. Blend the graham crackers with melted butter and 2 tablespoons sugar.
2. Place 1 heaping tablespoon of the mixture into jars and press slightly. Whisk cream cheese, sour cream, vanilla, lemon zest and sugar, until blended. Gradually whisk eggs, one at the time, until blended.
3. Spoon the mixture into jars, to ¾ full. Bake the mini caked for 30 minutes. Meanwhile microwave the jelly. Top cheesecakes with raspberries and pour over raspberry jelly. Cool and serve.

Nutrition Facts

Serving Size 98 g

Amount Per Serving

Calories 273	Calories from Fat 185
	% Daily Value*
Total Fat 20.6g	32%
Saturated Fat 12.3g	62%
Cholesterol 83mg	28%
Sodium 172mg	7%
Potassium 114mg	3%
Total Carbohydrates 18.6g	6%
Dietary Fiber 1.6g	6%
Sugars 11.7g	
Protein 4.9g	

Vitamin A 15%	•	Vitamin C 10%
Calcium 5%	•	Iron 6%

Nutrition Grade D-

* Based on a 2000 calorie diet

Cherry pie in jar

Serves: 4

Time: 60 minutes

Ingredients:

- 1 pie dough, store bought
- 1 tablespoon heavy cream
- 2 ½ cups sour cherries, pitted
- 1 ½ tablespoons cornstarch
- 1 teaspoon lemon juice
- ½ cup sugar
- Some sanding sugar

Directions:

1. Preheat oven to 375F.
2. Line the jars with pie dough, bottom and sides, stretching it slightly. Chill for 15 minutes.
3. Combine cherries with lemon juice in bowl. Combine sugar and cornstarch and sprinkle over cherries; toss to combine.
4. Fill the jars with cherries and bake for 15 minutes; cover and continue baking for 30 minutes more.
5. Roll out some more dough and cut out the circles, that will fit on the jar; make small cuts so steam can escape. Remove the jars from the oven and top with prepared dough rounds.
6. Brush dough with heavy cream and sprinkle with some sanding sugar. Top the pies with dough rounds and bake for 12-15 minutes more; serve at room temperature.

Nutrition Facts

Serving Size 122 g

Amount Per Serving

Calories 267	Calories from Fat 51
	% Daily Value*
Total Fat 5.7g	9%
Saturated Fat 2.4g	12%
Cholesterol 5mg	2%
Sodium 100mg	4%
Potassium 83mg	2%
Total Carbohydrates 54.9g	18%
Sugars 25.8g	
Protein 0.4g	
Vitamin A 4% •	Vitamin C 6%
Calcium 1% •	Iron 1%

Nutrition Grade D+

* Based on a 2000 calorie diet

Lazy cheesecake with lemon and strawberries

Serves: 6

Time: 15 minutes

Ingredients:

- 8oz. cream cheese, room temperature
- 8oz. sour cream
- 12oz. cool whip
- 3oz. lemon pudding
- 1 cup graham crackers, crushed
- 1 cup strawberries, mashed
- 1/3 cup butter, melted
- ½ cup milk
- 2 tablespoons sugar

Directions:

1. Combine sour cream, cool whip, cream cheese, pudding and milk in a bowl, until blended.
2. In separate bowl combine crackers, sugar and melted butter; mix until you get even mixture.
3. Divide half of the cracker mixture between the Mason jars; top with half of the cheese mixture and mashed strawberries; repeat layers and sprinkle with some crushed crackers on top.
4. Chill before serving.

Nutrition Facts

Serving Size 221 g

Amount Per Serving

Calories 629	Calories from Fat 429
	% Daily Value*
Total Fat 47.7g	73%
Saturated Fat 32.6g	163%
Cholesterol 87mg	29%
Sodium 517mg	22%
Potassium 182mg	5%
Total Carbohydrates 46.5g	15%
Dietary Fiber 0.9g	3%
Sugars 36.8g	
Protein 6.7g	

| Vitamin A 23% | • | Vitamin C 24% |
| Calcium 11% | • | Iron 6% |

Nutrition Grade D+

* Based on a 2000 calorie diet

Berry cream pie

Serves: 4

Time: 15 minutes

Ingredients:

- 2 cups heavy whipping cream, chilled
- 12 graham crackers, ground
- 2 cups raspberries, fresh
- 1 cup blueberries, fresh
- ½ cup strawberries, fresh, sliced
- ¼ cup coconut oil, melted
- ½ teaspoon vanilla paste

Directions:

1. Whip chilled cream to desired consistency; stir in vanilla paste and mix until blended.
2. Mash raspberries in a small bowl; place aside.
3. Combine graham crackers and melted coconut oil in a bowl, until blended thoroughly.
4. Divide the mashed raspberries between four wide mouth Mason jars; top with whipped cream, graham crackers – reserving some for the final layer.
5. Spread strawberry slices and blueberries and finally top with reserved whipped cream and remaining graham crumbs.
6. Chill before serving.

Nutrition Facts

Serving Size 231 g

Amount Per Serving

Calories 561	Calories from Fat 366
	% Daily Value*
Total Fat 40.6g	63%
Saturated Fat 26.3g	131%
Cholesterol 82mg	27%
Sodium 278mg	12%
Potassium 250mg	7%
Total Carbohydrates 47.9g	16%
Dietary Fiber 6.4g	26%
Sugars 20.3g	
Protein 5.3g	

| Vitamin A 18% | • | Vitamin C 55% |
| Calcium 7% | • | Iron 14% |

Nutrition Grade C+

* Based on a 2000 calorie diet

Peach cobbler in jar

Serves: 4

Time: 45 minutes

Ingredients:

- ½ cup milk
- ½ cup sugar
- ¼ cup butter, melted
- ½ cup bisquick mix
- 4 peaches, sliced

Directions:

1. Preheat oven to 375F and spray four Mason jars with some cooking oil.
2. Combine bisquick, milk and sugar; stir to combine. Add melted butter and stir well.
3. Place peaches in a jar and top with prepared batter.
4. Bake for 30-35 minutes; serve at room temperature.

Nutrition Facts

Serving Size 182 g

Amount Per Serving

Calories 310	Calories from Fat 132

	% Daily Value*
Total Fat 14.7g	23%
Saturated Fat 8.3g	41%
Trans Fat 0.6g	
Cholesterol 33mg	11%
Sodium 282mg	12%
Potassium 220mg	6%
Total Carbohydrates 45.7g	15%
Dietary Fiber 1.5g	6%
Sugars 35.0g	
Protein 3.1g	

Vitamin A 14%	Vitamin C 11%
Calcium 6%	Iron 4%

Nutrition Grade C-

* Based on a 2000 calorie diet

Banana split in jar

Serves: 2

Time: 10 minutes

Ingredients:

- 1 banana, medium, sliced
- 2/3 cup vanilla yogurt, frozen
- 2 tablespoons chocolate syrup
- 2 cherries, to garnish
- 4 tablespoons whipped topping

Directions:

1. Place the banana slices in two jars; top with yogurt.
2. Pour over chocolate syrup and whipped cream.
3. Garnish with cherries before serving.

Nutrition Facts

Serving Size 165 g

Amount Per Serving

Calories 178	Calories from Fat 25

	% Daily Value*
Total Fat 2.7g	4%
Saturated Fat 1.8g	9%
Cholesterol 9mg	3%
Sodium 79mg	3%
Potassium 453mg	13%
Total Carbohydrates 32.2g	11%
Dietary Fiber 2.0g	8%
Sugars 22.8g	
Protein 5.9g	

Vitamin A 3%	•	Vitamin C 10%
Calcium 16%	•	Iron 3%

Nutrition Grade B+

* Based on a 2000 calorie diet

Raspberry-Mascarpone cream dessert

Serves: 4

Time: 10 minutes + inactive time

Ingredients:

- 2 ½ cups raspberries, fresh
- 3 tablespoons powder sugar
- 1 tablespoon Limoncello
- ¾ cup heavy cream
- 1 cup mascarpone cheese

Directions:

1. Reserve 14 raspberries for the garnish.
2. Sprinkle powdered sugar over remaining raspberries and stir until melted. Place in refrigerator.
3. Combine Limoncello with mascarpone cheese and stir until blended.
4. Beat heavy cream until medium peaks form and stir in the mascarpone mixture.
5. Mash raspberries with fork and gently stir into cheese mixture; spoon the prepared cream into Mason jars and refrigerate for 50 minutes.
6. Top with reserved raspberries before serving.

Nutrition Facts

Serving Size 192 g

Amount Per Serving

Calories 314	Calories from Fat 152
	% Daily Value*
Total Fat 16.9g	26%
Saturated Fat 10.3g	52%
Cholesterol 62mg	21%
Sodium 61mg	3%
Potassium 198mg	6%
Total Carbohydrates 17.7g	6%
Dietary Fiber 5.0g	20%
Sugars 9.5g	
Protein 8.4g	

| Vitamin A 13% | • | Vitamin C 34% |
| Calcium 16% | • | Iron 4% |

Nutrition Grade B-

* Based on a 2000 calorie diet

Oreo cookie butter

Serves: 2

Time: 5 minutes

Ingredients:

- 10 Oreo cookies
- 1 ½ cups honey roasted peanuts

Directions:

1. Divide ingredients between two standard Mason jars.
2. Apply the blender base on one jars and process the ingredients until you get creamy consistency, for 3-4 minutes.
3. Repeat the process with remaining jar.
4. Serve with fresh apples or alone.

Nutrition Facts

Serving Size 158 g

Amount Per Serving

Calories 880	Calories from Fat 596
	% Daily Value*
Total Fat 66.2g	102%
Saturated Fat 11.2g	56%
Trans Fat 2.6g	
Cholesterol 0mg	0%
Sodium 587mg	24%
Potassium 878mg	25%
Total Carbohydrates 52.3g	17%
Dietary Fiber 11.6g	46%
Sugars 24.8g	
Protein 32.9g	

Vitamin A 0%	•	Vitamin C 1%
Calcium 8%	•	Iron 20%

Nutrition Grade B-

* Based on a 2000 calorie diet

Cherry crisp in jar

Serves: 4

Time: 30 minutes

Ingredients:

- 3 cups cherry pie filling
- ½ cup rolled oats
- ½ cup all-purpose flour
- ¼ cup butter, melted
- 1/3 cup brown sugar
- 2 tablespoons pecans, chopped

Directions:

1. Preheat oven to 350F and grease four Mason jars with some cooking oil.
2. Divide cherry pie filling between the jars.
3. In a medium bowl combine rolled oats, sugar, flour, pecans and melted butter; mix until blended.
4. Top the cherries with prepared topping and bake in preheated oven for 20-25 minutes.
5. Serve at room temperature.

Nutrition Facts

Serving Size 129 g

Amount Per Serving

Calories 373	Calories from Fat 156

	% Daily Value*
Total Fat 17.4g	27%
Saturated Fat 7.9g	40%
Cholesterol 31mg	10%
Sodium 99mg	4%
Potassium 176mg	5%
Total Carbohydrates 51.3g	17%
Dietary Fiber 2.6g	10%
Sugars 12.1g	
Protein 4.1g	

Vitamin A 10%	•	Vitamin C 4%
Calcium 3%	•	Iron 9%

Nutrition Grade C

* Based on a 2000 calorie diet

Chocolate cheesecake

Serves: 2

Time: 15 minutes + inactive time

Ingredients:

- 8oz. cream cheese
- 14oz. chocolate sweetened condensed milk
- Juice of ½ orange
- Zest of ½ orange
- 2oz. graham crackers, ground
- ¼ cup butter, melted
- 1 tablespoon sugar

Directions:

1. Combine ground crackers, sugar and butter in a bowl until blended.
2. Spoon in a wide mouth Mason jars and press to the bottom.
3. Combine cream cheese, chocolate milk, orange juice and zest.
4. Top the crust with prepared filling and refrigerate for 3 hours before serving.

Nutrition Facts

Serving Size 391 g

Amount Per Serving

Calories 1,351	Calories from Fat 657

	% Daily Value*
Total Fat 73.0g	112%
Saturated Fat 44.9g	224%
Trans Fat 0.0g	
Cholesterol 211mg	70%
Sodium 871mg	36%
Potassium 213mg	6%
Total Carbohydrates 152.9g	51%
Dietary Fiber 0.9g	4%
Sugars 136.6g	
Protein 26.0g	

Vitamin A 55%	•	Vitamin C 24%
Calcium 61%	•	Iron 15%

Nutrition Grade D+

* Based on a 2000 calorie diet

Grasshopper pies

Serves: 5

Time: 20 minutes + inactive time

Ingredients:

- 3 cups mini marshmallows
- 1 ½ cups whipping cream
- ½ cup milk
- 174 cup crème de Menthe
- 1 ½ cups coarsely chopped Oreo cookies (icing center removed)
- 2 tablespoons chocolate shavings

Directions:

1. Place the Oreos in food processor and pulse until coarsely ground.
2. In a sauce pan melt the marshmallows with milk, over medium heat.
3. Chill the mixture and stir in crème de Menthe.
4. Whip the whipping cream and stir in crème de Menthe mixture.
5. Spread cookies in Mason jars and press gently; spoon the crème de Menthe over cookies and sprinkle with chocolate shavings.
6. Chill for 2 hours before serving.

Nutrition Facts

Serving Size 117 g

Amount Per Serving

Calories 311	Calories from Fat 150
	% Daily Value*
Total Fat 16.7g	26%
Saturated Fat 9.8g	49%
Trans Fat 0.5g	
Cholesterol 42mg	14%
Sodium 97mg	4%
Potassium 69mg	2%
Total Carbohydrates 38.2g	13%
Dietary Fiber 1.2g	5%
Sugars 23.8g	
Protein 2.9g	

Vitamin A 7%	•	Vitamin C 0%
Calcium 6%	•	Iron 3%

Nutrition Grade D+

* Based on a 2000 calorie diet

Maple-pecan pie

Serves: 4

Time: 50 minutes

Ingredients:

- 8oz. pie crust
- 3 tablespoons rum
- ½ tablespoon cinnamon
- 7 tablespoons butter
- ½ cup brown sugar
- 3 eggs
- 1 ½ cup maple syrup
- 2 tablespoons sugar
- 1 tablespoon vanilla
- 2 cups pecans, chopped

Directions:

1. Preheat oven to 350F.
2. Roll the pie crust to ¼ -inch and line the four Mason jars with the dough, bottom and sides.
3. Bake crusts for 6 minutes; remove and place aside.
4. Bring maple syrup to boil in sauce pan; reduce heat and simmer until reduced by half.
5. Beat butter and sugars until creamy; add rum, eggs, vanilla and cinnamon; whisk until blended.
6. Stir in walnuts and reduced syrup, just until combined; divide the mixture between the jars.
7. Bake pies for 25-30 minutes; serve at room temperature.

Nutrition Facts

Serving Size 271 g

Amount Per Serving

Calories 941	Calories from Fat 340
	% Daily Value*
Total Fat 37.8g	58%
Saturated Fat 16.8g	84%
Trans Fat 0.0g	
Cholesterol 176mg	59%
Sodium 529mg	22%
Potassium 374mg	11%
Total Carbohydrates 141.4g	47%
Dietary Fiber 1.3g	5%
Sugars 116.3g	
Protein 6.8g	

| Vitamin A 25% | • | Vitamin C 0% |
| Calcium 14% | • | Iron 19% |

Nutrition Grade D-

* Based on a 2000 calorie diet

Monkey bread in jar

Serves: 4

Time: 20 minutes

Ingredients:

- ½ cup sugar
- 1 teaspoon ground cinnamon
- ½ cup brown sugar
- 10 refrigerated biscuits, cut into quarters

Directions:

1. Preheat oven to 350F and grease Mason jars with some cooking oil.
2. In a wide bowl combine sugars and cinnamon; coat the biscuits with sugar mixture.
3. Divide coated biscuits between the jars, adding extra sugar mixture as you go.
4. Fill the jar to ¾ and bake in preheated oven for 12-15 minutes. Serve at room temperature.

Nutrition Facts

Serving Size 96 g

Amount Per Serving

Calories 322	Calories from Fat 25

	% Daily Value*
Total Fat 2.7g	4%
Saturated Fat 0.7g	3%
Trans Fat 0.0g	
Cholesterol 0mg	0%
Sodium 767mg	32%
Potassium 124mg	4%
Total Carbohydrates 72.3g	24%
Dietary Fiber 1.3g	5%
Sugars 46.9g	
Protein 4.1g	

Vitamin A 0%	•	Vitamin C 0%
Calcium 3%	•	Iron 10%

Nutrition Grade B-

* Based on a 2000 calorie diet

Strawberry shortcake

Serves: 4

Time: 15 minutes

Ingredients:

- 1 yellow cake mix, baked according to package directions
- 8oz. whipped topping
- ¼ cup sugar
- 2 cups strawberries, fresh, sliced
- 8oz. can vanilla frosting

Directions:

1. Crumble cake mix and divide half between four Mason jars.
2. In a medium bowl whisk frosting and whipped topping; spoon small amount over cake.
3. Spoon half of the strawberries over frosting and repeat layers once more.
4. Serve immediately.

Nutrition Facts

Serving Size 141 g

Amount Per Serving

Calories 216	Calories from Fat 115

	% Daily Value*
Total Fat 12.8g	20%
Saturated Fat 7.8g	39%
Cholesterol 43mg	14%
Sodium 74mg	3%
Potassium 194mg	6%
Total Carbohydrates 25.1g	8%
Dietary Fiber 1.4g	6%
Sugars 20.6g	
Protein 2.3g	

Vitamin A 8%	•	Vitamin C 71%
Calcium 7%	•	Iron 2%

Nutrition Grade C

*Based on a 2000 calorie diet

Whiskey-chocolate cake

Serves: 4

Time: 60 minutes

Ingredients:

- 4 eggs, room temperature
- 1 cup brown sugar
- 1 stick butter
- ½ teaspoon baking soda
- ¼ teaspoon baking powder
- ½ cup whiskey
- 8oz. dark chocolate, chopped
- 4oz. softened butter
- 4oz. cream cheese
- 2 tablespoons whiskey

Directions:

1. Melt butter and chocolate in double boiler; stir well when melted and remove from the heat; stir in brown sugar.
2. Add whiskey and mix until combined; add eggs, one at the time, whisking after each addition; add baking soda and powder; mix well.
3. Spoon the batter into four jars and bake in preheated oven for 35 minutes at 375F. Meanwhile prepare the frosting; cream together cream cheese, butter and whiskey in a bowl.
4. Remove cakes from the oven and place aside to cool; when cool top with frosting before serving.

Nutrition Facts

Serving Size 229 g

Amount Per Serving

Calories 893	Calories from Fat 486
	% Daily Value*
Total Fat 54.0g	83%
Saturated Fat 33.9g	169%
Cholesterol 269mg	90%
Sodium 522mg	22%
Potassium 390mg	11%
Total Carbohydrates 70.5g	24%
Dietary Fiber 1.9g	8%
Sugars 64.8g	
Protein 12.3g	
Vitamin A 28%	Vitamin C 0%
Calcium 20%	Iron 16%

Nutrition Grade F

* Based on a 2000 calorie diet

Hot chocolate cupcakes

Serves: 5

Time: 40 minutes

Ingredients:

- 4 tablespoons butter, unsalted and room temperature
- 1 egg
- 3 tablespoons cocoa powder, raw
- 1 pinch salt
- ¾ teaspoon baking soda
- 3/ cup all-purpose flour
- 1/3 cup fresh brewed coffee
- 1/3 cup Greek yogurt
- 1 teaspoon vanilla
- ¾ cup sugar
- 1 cup whipped topping

Directions:

1. Preheat oven to 375F and coat five Mason jars with some cooking oil.
2. Cream the butter and sugar, in a bowl, until fluffy; add the egg and mix well.
3. Add vanilla, cocoa powder, salt and baking soda; mix until combined thoroughly.
4. Add flour and yogurt, in two parts and mix until blended completely.
5. Spoon the batter into jars, to 2/3 full and bake for 25 minutes. Allow to cool before topping with whipped topping. Serve after.

Nutrition Facts

Serving Size 102 g

Amount Per Serving

Calories 315	Calories from Fat 120

	% Daily Value*
Total Fat 13.3g	21%
Saturated Fat 8.0g	40%
Trans Fat 0.0g	
Cholesterol 66mg	22%
Sodium 315mg	13%
Potassium 143mg	4%
Total Carbohydrates 47.8g	16%
Dietary Fiber 1.5g	6%
Sugars 31.3g	
Protein 4.1g	

Vitamin A 8%	•	Vitamin C 0%	
Calcium 3%	•	Iron 9%	

Nutrition Grade D-

* Based on a 2000 calorie diet

No-bake cheesecake

Serves: 8

Time: 20 minutes + inactive time

Ingredients:

- 15 Oreo or any kind chocolate cookies, roughly chopped
- 8oz. cool whip
- 1 teaspoon vanilla
- 8oz. cream cheese
- ¾ cup sugar

Directions:

1. Chop the cookies and place aside.
2. Beta the cream cheese, cool whip, vanilla and sugar in a bowl; stir in chopped cookies.
3. Divide the mixture between eight Mason jars and refrigerate for 2 hours.
4. Serve after.

Nutrition Facts

Serving Size 140 g

Amount Per Serving

Calories 563 — Calories from Fat 264

	% Daily Value*
Total Fat 29.4g	45%
Saturated Fat 16.3g	82%
Trans Fat 0.0g	
Cholesterol 31mg	10%
Sodium 359mg	15%
Potassium 157mg	4%
Total Carbohydrates 72.0g	24%
Dietary Fiber 2.2g	9%
Sugars 51.1g	
Protein 4.7g	

Vitamin A 8% • Vitamin C 0%
Calcium 5% • Iron 19%

Nutrition Grade F

* Based on a 2000 calorie diet

Peanut butter-chocolate cupcakes

Serves: 12

Time: 40 minutes

Ingredients:

- 8oz. peanut butter
- 10oz. dark chocolate, quality
- 1 ½ cups powdered sugar
- 1 box Devils food cupcakes

Directions:

1. Preheat oven to 350F and spray 12 mini jars with some cooking spray.
2. Mix powder sugar and peanut butter until smooth. Make 1-inch balls from the mixture.
3. Prepare cupcake mix according to package directions; spoon the batter into jars and place in 1 peanut butter ball. Top with 2 tablespoons of batter.
4. Bake cupcakes for 15-20 minutes and remove from the oven. Melt dark chocolate over double boiler and pour over cupcakes; serve at room temperature.

Nutrition Facts

Serving Size 79 g

Amount Per Serving

Calories 376	Calories from Fat 167

	% Daily Value*
Total Fat 18.5g	29%
Saturated Fat 7.4g	37%
Trans Fat 0.0g	
Cholesterol 5mg	2%
Sodium 266mg	11%
Potassium 211mg	6%
Total Carbohydrates 48.8g	16%
Dietary Fiber 1.9g	8%
Sugars 37.7g	
Protein 6.5g	

Vitamin A 1%	•	Vitamin C 0%
Calcium 9%	•	Iron 19%

Nutrition Grade C

* Based on a 2000 calorie diet

Carrot cake in jar

Serves: 12

Time: 40 minutes

Ingredients:

- 1 ½ cups all-purpose flour
- 1 teaspoon cinnamon
- 1 large carrot, grated
- ½ cup walnuts, chopped
- 2 eggs
- 2 teaspoons baking soda
- ½ cup canola oil
- 1 cup sugar
- 2 teaspoons vanilla
- 1 teaspoon grated ginger, fresh
- ½ cup apple sauce
- 1 pinch salt

Directions:

1. Preheat oven to 350F and grease slightly 12 mini Mason jars; place aside.
2. Sift the flour, salt, cinnamon and baking soda in a bowl; in separate bowl whisk together the eggs, oil, vanilla, apple sauce and ginger. Fold the wet ingredients in dry ones and mix until just blended; stir in the carrot and walnuts.
3. Spoon the mixture into jars, to 2/3 full and bake for 30 minutes.
4. Cool before serving.

```
Nutrition Facts
Serving Size 66 g

Amount Per Serving
Calories 250                 Calories from Fat 117
                                       % Daily Value*
Total Fat 13.0g                              20%
  Saturated Fat 1.1g                          6%
  Trans Fat 0.0g
Cholesterol 27mg                              9%
Sodium 237mg                                 10%
Potassium 80mg                                2%
Total Carbohydrates 30.6g                    10%
  Dietary Fiber 1.1g                          4%
  Sugars 17.7g
Protein 3.8g

Vitamin A 21%          *       Vitamin C 1%
Calcium 1%             *       Iron 6%
Nutrition Grade C-
* Based on a 2000 calorie diet
```

Blueberry pies

Serves: 6

Time: 45 minutes

Ingredients:

- 8oz. pie dough
- 2 tablespoons butter
- 2 tablespoons flour
- ¾ cup white sugar
- ½ teaspoon cinnamon
- 4 cups fresh blueberries
- 1 teaspoon lemon zest, grated finely
- 1 egg, beaten
- Some sanding sugar

Directions:

1. Combine blueberries with sugar, flour, cinnamon and lemon zest in a bowl. Divide the mixture between six 4oz. Mason jars.
2. Cut the ¼ inch strips from the pie dough.
3. Top four strips across the jars and three more over the layered strips.
4. Brush the dough with egg and sprinkle with some sanding sugar; bake in preheated oven for 20 minutes at 375F.
5. Serve with some vanilla ice cream.

Nutrition Facts

Serving Size 175 g

Amount Per Serving

Calories 372	Calories from Fat 148
	% Daily Value*
Total Fat 16.4g	25%
Saturated Fat 6.7g	34%
Trans Fat 0.0g	
Cholesterol 37mg	12%
Sodium 268mg	11%
Potassium 90mg	3%
Total Carbohydrates 57.5g	19%
Dietary Fiber 2.5g	10%
Sugars 36.7g	
Protein 2.0g	

Vitamin A 3%	•	Vitamin C 26%
Calcium 1%	•	Iron 9%

Nutrition Grade C

* Based on a 2000 calorie diet

Pretzel-strawberry dessert

Serves: 10

Time: 20 minutes

Ingredients:

- 1 ½ cups pretzels, crushed
- 8oz. whipped topping
- 8oz. cream cheese
- 4 tablespoons white sugar
- 1 cup granulated sugar
- 1 teaspoon vanilla
- 6oz. flavored gelatin
- 2 cups water, boiling
- 16oz. strawberries, sliced
- 10 tablespoons butter, unsalted, softened

Directions:

1. Preheat oven to 350F.
2. In a bowl combine 4 tablespoons sugar, pretzels and butter; stir until combined.
3. Spoon 2 tablespoons of pretzel mixture into jars, pressing slightly. Bake the crust for 6 minutes; place aside to cool.
4. In a medium bowl cream together whipped topping, cream cheese and granulated sugar; divide the mixture between the jars and refrigerate for 1 hour.
5. Combine boiling water and gelatin powder; stir until gelatin is dissolved.
6. Stir in the strawberries and spoon the mixture over cream cheese mixture; place back jars in the fridge for 1 hour and serve after.

Nutrition Facts

Serving Size 203 g

Amount Per Serving

Calories 435	Calories from Fat 224
	% Daily Value*
Total Fat 24.8g	38%
Saturated Fat 15.5g	77%
Trans Fat 0.0g	
Cholesterol 73mg	24%
Sodium 322mg	13%
Potassium 148mg	4%
Total Carbohydrates 38.1g	13%
Dietary Fiber 1.1g	5%
Sugars 29.2g	
Protein 18.3g	

Vitamin A 16%	•	Vitamin C 44%
Calcium 6%	•	Iron 6%

Nutrition Grade D-

* Based on a 2000 calorie diet

Apple custard pie

Serves: 10 time: 40 minutes

Ingredients:

- 6 tablespoons butter
- 2 tablespoons sugar
- 1 tablespoon cinnamon
- 3 cups walnuts, ground
- 6 egg yolks
- 2 cups granulated sugar
- ¼ cup plain flour
- 1 cup heavy cream
- 4 cups diced apples

Directions:

1. Preheat oven to 425F and grease 10 mini Mason jars.
2. Place the walnuts, sugar and cinnamon in food processor; pulse until combined. Add butter and pulse until blended thoroughly. Spoon the mixture into jars; pressing down slightly.
3. Prepare the custard; beat the egg yolks, sugar, flour and heavy cream in a bowl; stir in apples and spoon the mixture over walnut crust.
4. Bake the pies for 12 minutes; reduce heat to 375F and bake further for 20 minutes more.
5. Serve at room temperature.

Nutrition Facts

Serving Size 158 g

Amount Per Serving

Calories 561	Calories from Fat 327
	% Daily Value*
Total Fat 36.3g	56%
Saturated Fat 9.4g	47%
Trans Fat 0.0g	
Cholesterol 161mg	54%
Sodium 60mg	2%
Potassium 271mg	8%
Total Carbohydrates 55.8g	19%
Dietary Fiber 4.0g	16%
Sugars 47.4g	
Protein 11.4g	

| Vitamin A 11% | • | Vitamin C 7% |
| Calcium 5% | • | Iron 10% |

Nutrition Grade C+

* Based on a 2000 calorie diet

Eclairs in jar

Serves: 4

Time: 20 minutes

Ingredients:

- 1 cup ground graham crackers
- 8oz. whipped topping
- 3 ½ cups milk
- 6oz. instant vanilla pudding
- 1 tub chocolate frosting

Directions:

1. Divide half of the graham crackers between four jars.
2. In large bowl combine pudding and milk; beat at medium speed, with electric mixer, for 2 minutes.
3. Fold in whipped topping and divide the mixture between the jars. Top with another layer of graham crackers and pour over chocolate frosting.
4. Refrigerate for 2 hours before serving.

Nutrition Facts

Serving Size 334 g

Amount Per Serving

Calories 502	Calories from Fat 174
	% Daily Value*
Total Fat 19.4g	30%
Saturated Fat 11.0g	55%
Cholesterol 61mg	20%
Sodium 914mg	38%
Potassium 239mg	7%
Total Carbohydrates 73.2g	24%
Dietary Fiber 0.6g	2%
Sugars 60.2g	
Protein 10.3g	

Vitamin A 9%	•	Vitamin C 0%
Calcium 32%	•	Iron 5%

Nutrition Grade C+

* Based on a 2000 calorie diet

Dark chocolate chips bread pudding

Serves: 6

Time: 30 minutes

Ingredients:

- 6 cups bread, torn into pieces
- 2 cups milk
- 2 teaspoons vanilla
- ½ cup sugar
- ¼ cup melted butter
- 2 eggs
- 1 cup dark chocolate chips

Directions:

1. Torn bread and place in large bowl; add chocolate chips and toss to combine.
2. Combine melted butter with vanilla, sugar, milk and eggs; whisk until blended.
3. Pour the milk mixture over bread and refrigerate for 1 hour.
4. Spray jars with some cooking oil and spoon the bread mixture into jars; bake for 25 minutes in preheated oven at 375F.
5. Serve at room temperature.

Nutrition Facts

Serving Size 179 g

Amount Per Serving

Calories 382 — Calories from Fat 156

	% Daily Value*
Total Fat 17.3g	27%
Saturated Fat 9.9g	49%
Cholesterol 82mg	27%
Sodium 352mg	15%
Potassium 106mg	3%
Total Carbohydrates 52.0g	17%
Dietary Fiber 0.8g	3%
Sugars 32.8g	
Protein 8.6g	

Vitamin A 7% • Vitamin C 0%
Calcium 16% • Iron 11%

Nutrition Grade D

* Based on a 2000 calorie diet

Banana pudding

Serves: 4

Time: 10 minutes

Ingredients:

- 1 cup Greek yogurt
- ½ teaspoon vanilla paste
- 8 wafer cookies
- 2 bananas, small, sliced
- ½ cup whipped topping
- 1 teaspoon cinnamon

Directions:

1. Place one wafer cookie in a jar; top with a layer of vanilla yogurt.
2. Add layer of banana slices and sprinkle with ¼ cinnamon. Top with whipped topping.
3. Repeat layers once more, finishing with whipped topping.
4. Serve immediately, or chilled.

Nutrition Facts

Serving Size 181 g

Amount Per Serving

Calories 376	Calories from Fat 153
	% Daily Value*
Total Fat 17.0g	26%
Saturated Fat 5.0g	25%
Trans Fat 0.0g	
Cholesterol 9mg	3%
Sodium 89mg	4%
Potassium 306mg	9%
Total Carbohydrates 51.2g	17%
Dietary Fiber 1.8g	7%
Sugars 10.1g	
Protein 6.6g	
Vitamin A 2%	Vitamin C 9%
Calcium 7%	Iron 5%

Nutrition Grade C-

* Based on a 2000 calorie diet

Baked fudge

Serves: 4

Time: 60 minutes

Ingredients:

- 2 eggs
- 1 cup sugar
- 1 teaspoon chocolate extract
- 1 teaspoon vanilla extract
- 1 teaspoon brown sugar
- 2 tablespoons cocoa powder, raw
- 2 tablespoons flour
- ½ cup butter, melted

Directions:

1. Preheat oven to 325F and grease four wide mouth Mason jars with cooking spray.
2. Beat the eggs until pale; add sugars and beat until combined.
3. Add the extracts, butter and flour; beat until combined.
4. Pour the butter into jars and place them into baking dish; pour over 1 cup boiling water.
5. Bake the fudge for 40-45 minutes.
6. Serve at room temperature.

Nutrition Facts

Serving Size 109 g

Amount Per Serving

Calories 449	Calories from Fat 230
	% Daily Value*
Total Fat 25.6g	39%
Saturated Fat 15.5g	77%
Cholesterol 143mg	48%
Sodium 195mg	8%
Potassium 111mg	3%
Total Carbohydrates 55.5g	19%
Dietary Fiber 0.9g	4%
Sugars 51.1g	
Protein 3.9g	
Vitamin A 16%	Vitamin C 0%
Calcium 2%	Iron 6%

Nutrition Grade F

* Based on a 2000 calorie diet

Italian caramel pudding

Serves: 4

Ingredients:

- ¼ cup sugar
- ½ pint milk
- 2 eggs
- ¼ cup sugar – for the caramel
- 1 vanilla pod, seeds scraped
- ½ teaspoon lemon juice
- Small pinch of salt

Directions:

1. Place sugar in sauce pan with lemon juice and salt; heat over medium-low heat.
2. Heat until sugar dissolves and caramel forms.
3. Pour caramel in four wide mouth Mason jars.
4. Gently heat milk in another sauce pan and add vanilla seeds.
5. Beat 1 egg and just 1 egg yolk with remaining sugar, until well whisked.
6. Gradually add milk in the egg mixture and whisk constantly, until all milk is incorporated.
7. Preheat oven to 130C/265F.
8. Pour the milk on top of caramel and place the jars in larger dish filled with water.
9. Bake for 1 hour and allow cooling before serving.

Nutrition Facts

Serving Size 109 g

Amount Per Serving

Calories 156	Calories from Fat 31

	% Daily Value*
Total Fat 3.4g	5%
Saturated Fat 1.4g	7%
Cholesterol 87mg	29%
Sodium 60mg	2%
Potassium 65mg	2%
Total Carbohydrates 28.2g	9%
Sugars 27.9g	
Protein 4.8g	

Vitamin A 2%	Vitamin C 0%
Calcium 8%	Iron 2%

Nutrition Grade B-

* Based on a 2000 calorie diet

Pumpkin-coffee pie in jar

Serves: 1

Time: 5 minutes

Ingredients:

- ¼ cup all-purpose flour + 2 tablespoons
- 2 tablespoons butter
- 3 tablespoons brown sugar
- 2 tablespoons pumpkin puree
- 1/8 teaspoon baking soda
- ¼ teaspoon cinnamon
- Pinch of ground cloves
- ½ teaspoon instant coffee

Directions:

1. In a standard Mason jar soften 1 tablespoon of butter in microwave, for 5 seconds.
2. Stir in 2 tablespoons sugar and stir until combined.
3. Stir in vanilla, pumpkin, instant coffee, flour, baking powder, salt and cloves.
4. Stir until just combined.
5. Prepare the streusel; in a separate bowl combine 2 tablespoons flour, cinnamon and remaining butter.
6. Mix the ingredients with fingers until you have crumbly mixture.
7. Set on top of prepared cake and microwave for 60 seconds.
8. Serve while still warm.

Nutrition Facts

Serving Size 121 g

Amount Per Serving

Calories 433 — Calories from Fat 212

	% Daily Value*
Total Fat 23.5g	36%
Saturated Fat 14.7g	73%
Trans Fat 0.0g	
Cholesterol 61mg	20%
Sodium 333mg	14%
Potassium 146mg	4%
Total Carbohydrates 53.5g	18%
Dietary Fiber 2.1g	9%
Sugars 27.3g	
Protein 3.9g	

Vitamin A 110%	Vitamin C 3%
Calcium 5%	Iron 12%

Nutrition Grade C

* Based on a 2000 calorie diet

Coconut simple cake

Serves: 1

Time: 10 minutes

Ingredients:

- 1 egg
- ½ teaspoon vanilla extract
- ¼ teaspoon coconut extract
- 2 tablespoons coconut milk
- ½ tablespoon honey
- 1 ½ tablespoons coconut flour
- 1 tablespoon cocoa powder
- 1 tablespoon coconut thick cream
- 1 teaspoon toasted shredded coconut

Directions:

1. Combine egg and milk in a standard Mason jar, using fork until well blended.
2. Add remaining ingredients and stir with fork until coconut flour is well incorporated.
3. Microwave for 1 minute 40 seconds.
4. Top with coconut cream and shredded coconut before serving.

Nutrition Facts

Serving Size 205 g

Amount Per Serving

Calories 236　　　　　Calories from Fat 129

	% Daily Value*
Total Fat 14.3g	22%
Saturated Fat 10.1g	51%
Trans Fat 0.0g	
Cholesterol 164mg	55%
Sodium 91mg	4%
Potassium 289mg	8%
Total Carbohydrates 20.3g	7%
Dietary Fiber 6.2g	25%
Sugars 11.3g	
Protein 8.8g	

Vitamin A 4%	•	Vitamin C 2%
Calcium 4%	•	Iron 21%

Nutrition Grade C

* Based on a 2000 calorie diet

Blackberry cream pie

Serves: 6

Time: 30 minutes

Ingredients:

- 30 shortbread cookies
- 1/3 cup blackberry juice
- 3 tablespoons butter, melted
- ½ cup blackberry jam, seedless
- 2 cups cool whip
- ½ cup blackberries, fresh

Directions:

1. Place cookies in food processor and pulse until finely ground; add butter and process until blended thoroughly.
2. Divide the cookie mixture between the jars; press slightly with a clean wine cork.
3. Whisk jam and blackberry juice in large bowl; add cool whip and mix until blended.
4. Spoon over cookie crusts.
5. Refrigerate for 1 hour and garnish with fresh blackberries before serving.

Nutrition Facts

Serving Size 97 g

Amount Per Serving

Calories 274   Calories from Fat 145

	% Daily Value*
Total Fat 16.1g	25%
Saturated Fat 11.4g	57%
Cholesterol 26mg	9%
Sodium 77mg	3%
Potassium 42mg	1%
Total Carbohydrates 32.6g	11%
Dietary Fiber 0.8g	3%
Sugars 26.0g	
Protein 1.1g	

Vitamin A 5%   •   Vitamin C 4%
Calcium 1%   •   Iron 1%

Nutrition Grade D

* Based on a 2000 calorie diet

Lemon raspberry mousse pie

Serves: 2

Time: 20 minutes + inactive time

Ingredients:

- 6oz. vanilla cool whip
- ¾ cup raspberry pie filling
- ½ cup lemon pie filling
- 6 sheets graham crackers, ground
- 2 tablespoons butter, melted
- ¼ cup fresh raspberries

Directions:

1. Combine graham crackers and butter in a bowl, until blended thoroughly.
2. Combine cool whip and raspberry pie filling in a bowl.
3. Place two tablespoons of graham cookie mixture in each jar; precisely two jars.
4. Top with ½ cup raspberry mousse and 2 tablespoons lemon pie filling.
5. Repeat lasers and chill in refrigerator for 1 hour before serving.
6. Garnish with fresh raspberries.

Nutrition Facts

Serving Size 282 g

Amount Per Serving

Calories 480 — Calories from Fat 193

	% Daily Value*
Total Fat 21.5g	33%
Saturated Fat 16.7g	84%
Trans Fat 0.0g	
Cholesterol 42mg	14%
Sodium 288mg	12%
Potassium 27mg	1%
Total Carbohydrates 73.5g	24%
Dietary Fiber 3.3g	13%
Sugars 33.1g	
Protein 0.3g	

Vitamin A 7%	•	Vitamin C 7%
Calcium 3%	•	Iron 4%

Nutrition Grade D

* Based on a 2000 calorie diet

Raisins and yogurt cake

Serves: 1

Time: 5minutes

Ingredients:

- 1 ½ tablespoon butter, room temperature
- 1 egg
- 3 tablespoons yogurt
- ¼ teaspoon vanilla extract
- 1 tablespoon raisins
- 4 tablespoons all-purpose flour
- ½ teaspoon baking soda
- 2 tablespoons sugar

Directions:

1. Cream the butter and sugar in a bowl.
2. Add remaining ingredients and stir well with fork, until smooth. Transfer into standard jar.
3. Microwave the cake for 3 minutes or until firm to the touch.
4. Dust with icing sugar before serving.

Nutrition Facts

Serving Size 179 g

Amount Per Serving

Calories 482　　　　Calories from Fat 203

　　　　　　　　　　　　　　　% Daily Value*

Total Fat 22.6g	35%
Saturated Fat 12.8g	64%
Cholesterol 212mg	71%
Sodium 847mg	35%
Potassium 274mg	8%
Total Carbohydrates 58.7g	20%
Dietary Fiber 1.2g	5%
Sugars 33.1g	
Protein 11.8g	

Vitamin A 15%	Vitamin C 1%
Calcium 12%	Iron 14%

Nutrition Grade D+

* Based on a 2000 calorie diet

Cherry-chocolate cake

Serves: 1

Time: 5 minutes

Ingredients:

- 2 tablespoons dark chocolate chips
- 2 tablespoons cherry compote
- 1 egg
- 1 ripe banana
- 1 tablespoon almond butter
- 2 tablespoons cocoa, unsweetened
- ¼ teaspoon pure vanilla
- 2-3 drops stevia

Directions:

1. Mash the banana in a standard Mason jar using a fork.
2. Add remaining ingredients and stir well to combine.
3. Microwave for 2-3 minutes or until firm to the touch.
4. Dust with some cocoa powder before serving.

Nutrition Facts

Serving Size 229 g

Amount Per Serving

Calories 364	Calories from Fat 173

	% Daily Value*
Total Fat 19.2g	30%
Saturated Fat 5.7g	28%
Cholesterol 164mg	55%
Sodium 65mg	3%
Potassium 874mg	25%
Total Carbohydrates 46.0g	15%
Dietary Fiber 6.9g	28%
Sugars 23.0g	
Protein 13.2g	

Vitamin A 6%	•	Vitamin C 17%
Calcium 8%	•	Iron 21%

Nutrition Grade B

* Based on a 2000 calorie diet

Crème brulee with ginger

Serves: 6

Time: 35 minutes + inactive time

Ingredients:

- 7 egg yolks
- ½ teaspoon vanilla extract
- 3 cups heavy cream
- 1/3 cup + 2 tablespoons white sugar, divided
- 3 tablespoons brown sugar
- 1 teaspoon finely ground ginger

Directions:

1. Heat the oven to 350F and prepare six mini Mason jars.
2. Beat the egg yolks with half of the white sugar and vanilla, until thick and creamy.
3. Transfer the cream into sauce pan, add ginger and heat over medium heat until it almost come to boil. Stir the heavy cream into egg mixture and whisk until combined.
4. Now, pour the mixture into the top of double boiler. You can also drain it through sieve if you want to remove ginger pieces. Stir for 3 minutes and pour into prepared jars.
5. Bake for 30 minutes in preheated oven and set on wire rack to cool. Refrigerate for 1 hour.
6. When chilled enough, sprinkle with remaining white and brown sugar.
7. Preheat oven to broil; place the sprinkle custard under broiler for 2 minutes or until the sugar melts. Place again to cool and refrigerate for hour more. Serve at the room temperature.

Nutrition Facts

Serving Size 85 g

Amount Per Serving

Calories 289	Calories from Fat 247

	% Daily Value*
Total Fat 27.5g	42%
Saturated Fat 15.7g	79%
Cholesterol 327mg	109%
Sodium 34mg	1%
Potassium 77mg	2%
Total Carbohydrates 7.0g	2%
Sugars 4.6g	
Protein 4.4g	

Vitamin A 23%	•	Vitamin C 1%
Calcium 7%	•	Iron 3%

Nutrition Grade D

* Based on a 2000 calorie diet

After Eight mini cakes

Serves: 6

Time: 20 minutes

Ingredients:

- 5 oz. semisweet chocolate
- 8 tablespoons unsalted butter
- ½ cup brown rice flour
- 1 ½ cups powdered sugar
- 3 egg + 3 egg yolks, whisked
  4 oz. semisweet chocolate
- 2 oz. unsweetened chocolate, chopped
- 1 small teaspoon peppermint extract
- 2 tablespoons honey
- 1/3 cup hot water

Directions:

1. The sauce; Melt chocolate over steam or double boiler.
2. Add hot water, honey and peppermint extract.
3. Whisk until smooth and remove from the heat; set aside to cool.
4. Meanwhile prepare the lava cakes; Preheat oven to 450F and coat 6 mini jars with butter.
5. Melt remaining butter and chocolate in sauce pan over low heat; set aside to cool slightly.
6. Whisk the eggs in a bowl with sugar, until fluffy. Add brown rice flour, chocolate mixture and pour the batter into ramekins. Bake the cakes in preheated oven for 10-12. Cool slightly an pour over mint sauce. Serve immediately.

Nutrition Facts

Serving Size 165 g

Amount Per Serving

Calories 631	Calories from Fat 341
	% Daily Value*
Total Fat 37.9g	58%
Saturated Fat 21.9g	109%
Cholesterol 227mg	76%
Sodium 153mg	6%
Potassium 319mg	9%
Total Carbohydrates 75.9g	25%
Dietary Fiber 4.7g	19%
Sugars 58.7g	
Protein 8.2g	
Vitamin A 14% •	Vitamin C 0%
Calcium 5% •	Iron 22%

Nutrition Grade C

* Based on a 2000 calorie diet

Ice cream pie

Serves: 6

Time: 40 minutes + inactive time

- 2 cups wafer cookies
- ½ cup butter, melted + 1 tablespoon
- ¾ cup whipped cream
- 8 tablespoons coffee liqueur
- 1 teaspoon instant espresso
- 1 pint coconut ice cream
- 1 pint chocolate ice cream
- 4 oz. bitter-sweet chocolate
- 1 tablespoon amaretto

Directions:

1. Preheat oven to 325F and slightly grease six wide mouth Mason jars.
2. In a medium bowl combine melted butter and crushed cookies; spread evenly into jars and press with fingers around edges.
3. Bake the crust in oven for 10-12 minutes and set on wire rack to cool.
4. Heat 6 tablespoons of liqueur in small sauce pan and combine with instant coffee. Stir until coffee dissolves; add chopped chocolate and remaining butter. Place aside to cool.
5. In separate bowl combine coconut ice cream and 1 tablespoon coffee liqueur, using electric hand mixer. Spread the prepared ice cream over cooled crust and freeze until firm.
6. Combine chocolate ice cream with remaining coffee liqueur and amaretto, using electric mixer.
7. Spread chocolate mixture over coconut mixture and set in freezer until firm.
8. Serve when chilled thoroughly and garnish with whipping cream.

Nutrition Facts

Serving Size 175 g

Amount Per Serving

Calories 1,698   Calories from Fat 1247

	% Daily Value*
Total Fat 138.6g	213%
Saturated Fat 84.0g	420%
Trans Fat 0.0g	
Cholesterol 100mg	33%
Sodium 388mg	16%
Potassium 217mg	6%
Total Carbohydrates 142.0g	47%
Dietary Fiber 22.3g	89%
Sugars 92.6g	
Protein 20.1g	

Vitamin A 21%	•	Vitamin C 1%
Calcium 25%	•	Iron 109%

Nutrition Grade F

* Based on a 2000 calorie diet

Butterscotch lava cake

Serves: 6

Time: 25 minutes

Ingredients:

- ½ cup almond flour
- 6 tablespoon crushed crackers
- 6 oz. butterscotch chips
- 2/3 cup butter
- 3 eggs, room temperature
- Dash of salt
- 3 egg yolks
- ¾ cup brown sugar

Directions:

1. Preheat oven to 450F and slightly grease six 6 oz. Mason jars with oil and sprinkle with 1 tablespoon of crushed crackers at the bottom and sides, per jar.
2. In a small sauce pan melt chips and butter over medium-high heat, stirring constantly until dissolves.
3. Set aside to cool for 5 minutes.
4. In a large bowl whisk eggs and egg yolks with electric whisk until well combined.
5. Whisk sugar, butterscotch mixer and flour until well blended.
6. Divide the batter between custard cups and set them on baking tray.
7. Bake for 12-14 minutes or until top is puffed and cracked. Serve while still warm.

Nutrition Facts

Serving Size 111 g

Amount Per Serving

Calories 432	Calories from Fat 243
	% Daily Value*
Total Fat 27.0g	42%
Saturated Fat 15.1g	76%
Cholesterol 244mg	81%
Sodium 324mg	14%
Potassium 70mg	2%
Total Carbohydrates 44.4g	15%
Sugars 40.7g	
Protein 4.9g	

Vitamin A 18%	•	Vitamin C 0%
Calcium 5%	•	Iron 5%

Nutrition Grade D+

* Based on a 2000 calorie diet

Pumpkin panna cotta

Serves: 6

Time: 35 minutes + inactive time

Ingredients:

- 2 ¼ teaspoons gelatin, powdered and unflavored
- 1 ¾ cups heavy cream
- ¼ cup + 2 tablespoons brown sugar
- ½ teaspoon vanilla
- ½ teaspoon ground cinnamon
- ¾ cup pumpkin puree
- ¾ cup almond milk
- 1 apple, medium
- ¼ cup light honey
- ½ vanilla bean, seeds scraped
- 1/3 cup apple cider
- 1 cup sugar

Directions:

1. Peel and core the apple and chop in small dices.
2. Combine the honey, sugar and ½ cup of water in small sauce pan. Add scraped vanilla seeds and heat all over medium heat. Cook for 8 minutes or until sugar begins to turn gold around the edges. Stir in the apples and continue cooking for 3-5 minutes more.
3. Remove from the heat and slowly stir in the cider, salt and vinegar.
4. Set aside and prepare the panna cotta; in a small bowl combine gelatin and ¼ cup water.
5. Whisk the milk, cream, sugar and salt in a sauce pan and heat over medium-high heat, until just starts to boil. Remove from the heat and stir in the gelatin. Add pumpkin puree and strain entire mixture in a bowl through a fine sieve. Divide between six mini Mason jars and cover each with plastic foil. Refrigerate for 4 hours. Serve panna cotta with apple sauce on top.

Nutrition Facts

Serving Size 180 g

Amount Per Serving

Calories 353	Calories from Fat 183
	% Daily Value*
Total Fat 20.3g	31%
Saturated Fat 14.5g	72%
Trans Fat 0.0g	
Cholesterol 48mg	16%
Sodium 47mg	2%
Potassium 221mg	6%
Total Carbohydrates 45.2g	15%
Dietary Fiber 2.4g	10%
Sugars 40.8g	
Protein 1.9g	

| Vitamin A 106% | • | Vitamin C 8% |
| Calcium 4% | • | Iron 6% |

Nutrition Grade D

* Based on a 2000 calorie diet

Almond and orange cake

Serves: 6

Time: 40 minutes

Ingredients:

- 2/3 cup almond paste
- 1 cup sugar
- 1 vanilla bean, seeds scraped
- 4 eggs, room temperature
- ¼ cup millet flour
- ½ teaspoon baking soda
- 5 tablespoon ghee, melted and cooled
- 1 lb. oranges, seeded and thinly sliced
- 1 teaspoon orange zest
- 1 teaspoon lemon zest
- ½ cup water

Directions:

1. Preheat oven to 350F and prepare six wide Mouth jars.
2. Combine ½ cup of water and sugar in sauce pan. Add vanilla seeds and bring to boil over high heat. Reduce the heat to medium and simmer until sugar is dissolved.
3. Add orange slices and cook for 10 minutes, remove from the heat and set aside leaving the oranges in syrup. Combine one egg, orange zest, lemon zest and almond paste with hand mixer, until combined. Add remaining eggs and mix on high until pale and fluffy. Add the baking soda, millet flour and melted ghee; mix for 30 seconds or until combined.
4. Pour the batter in prepared jars and bake for 30 minutes. Let it cool for 15-20 minutes and top with candied oranges; serve.

Nutrition Facts

Serving Size 201 g

Amount Per Serving

Calories 434	Calories from Fat 188
	% Daily Value*
Total Fat 20.9g	32%
Saturated Fat 8.2g	41%
Trans Fat 0.0g	
Cholesterol 136mg	45%
Sodium 148mg	6%
Potassium 283mg	8%
Total Carbohydrates 59.0g	20%
Dietary Fiber 3.6g	14%
Sugars 49.8g	
Protein 7.4g	
Vitamin A 13% •	Vitamin C 68%
Calcium 9% •	Iron 8%

Nutrition Grade C+

* Based on a 2000 calorie diet

Butter pudding cakes

Serves: 6

Time: 40 minutes + inactive time

Ingredients:

- ¼ cup unsalted butter + some more to coat the ramekins
- 3 eggs, separated
- ¼ cup almond flour
- Dash of salt
- 1 1/3 cup + 1 tablespoon milk
- 1 teaspoon vanilla
- ¼ cup sugar
- 2/3 cup packed brown sugar
- 3 tablespoons rum (or 1 teaspoon extract for kid friendly version)

Directions:

1. Preheat oven to 350F and coat six 6 oz. Mason jars with butter and set on baking pan.
2. Melt the butter in microwave and whisk it with a sugar in a bowl. Add egg yolks and whisk using electric whisk until fluffy. Add almond flour, salt and some of the milk, so flour can easily be mixed. Whisk in the remaining milk, vanilla and rum; until smooth. Set aside.
3. Whisk the egg whites in a bowl, using electric whisk until soft peaks form.
4. Reduce the whisk speed to medium and while still running add sugar. Continue whisking until firm peaks form. Add 1/3 of the egg whites in egg yolk mixture and combine gently.
5. Add remaining egg whites and gently stir to combine it all.
6. Transfer the mixture into prepared ramekins and bake for 25-30 minutes or until the tops are light golden. Carefully remove them from the baking pan in cold water bath.
7. When the reach room temperature set them in refrigerator for 2 hours. Serve after.

Nutrition Facts

Serving Size 122 g

Amount Per Serving	
Calories 244	Calories from Fat 104
	% Daily Value*
Total Fat 11.5g	18%
Saturated Fat 6.2g	31%
Cholesterol 107mg	36%
Sodium 143mg	6%
Potassium 86mg	2%
Total Carbohydrates 27.3g	9%
Sugars 26.7g	
Protein 4.9g	
Vitamin A 7%	Vitamin C 0%
Calcium 9%	Iron 3%

Nutrition Grade D

* Based on a 2000 calorie diet

Baked chocolate mousse

Serves: 6

Time: 30 minutes

Ingredients:

- 3 tablespoons pure cocoa
- ¼ cup water
- 3 tablespoons sugar
- ½ teaspoon espresso granules
- 2 oz. bitter sweet chocolate
- 0.5 oz. unsweetened chocolate
- ¼ teaspoon vanilla extract
- ½ tablespoon white rum
- Dash of salt
- 1 cup whipping cream, whipped
- 1 egg + 1 egg white

Directions:

1. Preheat oven to 350F and spray 6 wide mouth Mason jars with cooking oil.
2. Bring water to boil in sauce pan over medium heat. Stir in the cocoa and continue stirring until dissolves. Add chocolates, coffee and stir as well. Transfer the mixture into a bowl and set aside; stir occasionally to avoid that crust that may form.
3. Make double boiler with pot of boiling water and oven proof bowl ate the top. Add the egg. Egg white and sugar in oven proof bow and whisk constantly for 2 minutes.
4. Remove the oven proof bowl from the heat, and using electric whisk, whisk the eggs until fluffy. Fold the eggs into chocolate and stir gently until well mixed. Add whipped cream and stir again, until well incorporated.
5. Transfer the mixture into prepared jars and bake for 25-28 minutes.
6. Set on wire rack to cool, then transfer to the refrigerator and chill for 4 hours; serve after.

Nutrition Facts

Serving Size 60 g

Amount Per Serving

Calories 171	Calories from Fat 106
	% Daily Value*
Total Fat 11.7g	18%
Saturated Fat 7.3g	37%
Cholesterol 52mg	17%
Sodium 25mg	1%
Potassium 84mg	2%
Total Carbohydrates 13.5g	5%
Dietary Fiber 1.8g	7%
Sugars 11.0g	
Protein 3.1g	

| Vitamin A 5% | • | Vitamin C 0% |
| Calcium 4% | • | Iron 4% |

Nutrition Grade D

*Based on a 2000 calorie diet

Fast peanut butter and chocolate cake

Serves: 1

Time: 10 minutes

Ingredients:

- ¼ cup all-purpose flour
- ¼ teaspoon baking powder
- ¼ cup milk
- 1 tablespoon creamy peanut butter
- 1 tablespoon mini chocolate chips
- 2 tablespoons melted and cooled butter
- 2 tablespoons unsweetened cocoa powder
- 2 tablespoons brown sugar
- ¼ teaspoon vanilla

Directions:

1. In a standard Mason jar combine flour, baking powder, sugar and cocoa powder.
2. Blend in milk, butter and vanilla until batter is smooth.
3. Combine peanut butter and chocolate chips in dollop and place in the center of mug, pressing down until even with the batter.
4. Microwave for 1 minute on high.
5. Allow to cool slightly before serving.

Nutrition Facts

Serving Size 139 g

Amount Per Serving

Calories 336	Calories from Fat 100

	% Daily Value*
Total Fat 11.1g	17%
Saturated Fat 3.4g	17%
Cholesterol 5mg	2%
Sodium 111mg	5%
Potassium 489mg	14%
Total Carbohydrates 54.2g	18%
Dietary Fiber 5.4g	22%
Sugars 22.1g	
Protein 11.4g	

Vitamin A 0%	•	Vitamin C 0%
Calcium 16%	•	Iron 26%

Nutrition Grade C+

* Based on a 2000 calorie diet

Sweet potato cake in jar

Serves: 6

Time: 30 minutes

Ingredients:

- 1 cup all-purpose flour
- 1 teaspoon baking soda
- 1 teaspoon ground cinnamon
- 1 cup sugar
- 2 eggs
- 1 cup vegetable oil
- 1 teaspoon vanilla extract
- ¼ teaspoon all spice
- ¼ teaspoon ground nutmeg
- 1 ½ cups shredded sweet potatoes
- ½ cup chopped walnuts
- 4 oz. cream cheese
- ¼ cup butter, softened
- ½ teaspoon vanilla extract
- 1 cup confectioners' sugar

Directions:

1. Preheat oven to 350F and grease six wide mouth Mason jars with some oil.
2. In a large bowl whisk eggs, oil, vanilla and sugar until well blended.
3. In separate bowl whisk dry ingredients; fold dry mixture into egg mixture and stir until just combined. Stir in walnuts and sweet potatoes and stir until well combined.
4. Transfer the mixture into prepared pan and bake for 40 minutes or until inserted toothpick comes out clean. Set on wire rack to cool completely.
5. Meanwhile, prepare the frosting; cream sugar, cheese and butter until blended.

6. Gradually add sugar until well incorporated. Spread the frosting over cooled cake; serve,

Nutrition Facts

Serving Size 184 g

Amount Per Serving	
Calories 790	Calories from Fat 526
	% Daily Value*
Total Fat 58.5g	90%
Saturated Fat 17.0g	85%
Trans Fat 0.0g	
Cholesterol 96mg	32%
Sodium 346mg	14%
Potassium 431mg	12%
Total Carbohydrates 61.8g	21%
Dietary Fiber 3.0g	12%
Sugars 34.0g	
Protein 8.6g	

Vitamin A 12%	•	Vitamin C 11%	
Calcium 5%	•	Iron 11%	

Nutrition Grade D-

*Based on a 2000 calorie diet

Almond cake in jar

Serves: 6

Time: 40 minutes

Ingredients:

- ½ lb. whole almonds, blanched and ground
- 4 drops pure almond extract
- 2 drops orange extract
- 1 ¼ cup fine sugar
- Grated zest of 1 lemon
- Grated zest of 1 orange
- 6 eggs, separated
- Some icing sugar -to dust

Directions:

1. Preheat oven to 350F.
2. Separate the eggs and whisk the egg yolks with sugar until pale; whisk in the zests and orange and almond extract. Gradually add the almond flour stirring well until blended.
3. Whisk egg whites, using electric whisk, until soft peaks form.
4. Brush six s07. Mason jars with some butter.
5. Transfer the batter into prepared pan and bake for 40 minutes or until firm to the touch. Set on wire rack to cool before slicing. Dust the cake with icing sugar before serving; serve when cooled.

Nutrition Facts

Serving Size 164 g

Amount Per Serving

Calories 455	Calories from Fat 210
	% Daily Value*
Total Fat 23.3g	36%
Saturated Fat 2.8g	14%
Trans Fat 0.0g	
Cholesterol 164mg	55%
Sodium 62mg	3%
Potassium 405mg	12%
Total Carbohydrates 54.6g	18%
Dietary Fiber 5.7g	23%
Sugars 46.7g	
Protein 13.9g	

Vitamin A 6%	•	Vitamin C	36%
Calcium 14%	•	Iron	13%

Nutrition Grade B

* Based on a 2000 calorie diet

Mango float

Serves: 4

Time: 30 minutes

Ingredients:

- 2 ripe mangoes, sliced into strips
- 3 tablespoons graham crackers, crushed
- 4 wafers
- ¾ cup condensed milk
- ½ cup thick cream

Directions:

1. Combine thick cream and condensed milk in a bowl.
2. Place wafers in mini Mason jars, one per jar. Add layer of milk mixture, followed with mango.
3. Repeat layers with mango and milk, finishing with a layer of ground crackers.
4. Chill and serve.

Nutrition Facts

Serving Size 179 g

Amount Per Serving

Calories 400 — Calories from Fat 105

	% Daily Value*
Total Fat 11.6g	18%
Saturated Fat 4.8g	24%
Trans Fat 0.0g	
Cholesterol 25mg	8%
Sodium 213mg	9%
Potassium 381mg	11%
Total Carbohydrates 69.7g	23%
Dietary Fiber 1.6g	7%
Sugars 56.2g	
Protein 6.2g	

Vitamin A 16% • Vitamin C 42%
Calcium 19% • Iron 6%

Nutrition Grade B-

* Based on a 2000 calorie diet

Banana whipped cream and strawberries dessert

Serves: 2

Time: 10 minutes

Ingredients:

- 1 ripe banana
- 1 ¼ cup whipping cream
- 1 tablespoon superfine icing
- 2 teaspoons vanilla extract
- 6 lady fingers
- ½ cup strawberries, halved

Directions:

1. In small bowl mash the bananas.
2. In separate bowl whip the cream, sugar and vanilla until soft peaks form.
3. Fold in mashed bananas until completely blended.
4. Break three lady fingers per jar; top with strawberries and spoon or pipe over banana cream.
5. Chill or serve immediately.

Nutrition Facts

Serving Size 199 g

Amount Per Serving

Calories 378	Calories from Fat 215
	% Daily Value*
Total Fat 23.9g	37%
Saturated Fat 14.6g	73%
Cholesterol 98mg	33%
Sodium 72mg	3%
Potassium 345mg	10%
Total Carbohydrates 37.8g	13%
Dietary Fiber 2.2g	9%
Sugars 19.3g	
Protein 4.0g	

| Vitamin A 16% | • | Vitamin C 45% |
| Calcium 6% | • | Iron 2% |

Nutrition Grade D

* Based on a 2000 calorie diet

Butterscotch crème

Serves: 6

Time: 60 minutes

Ingredients:

- 4 egg yolks
- 6 tablespoons dark sugar
- 1 ½ cups heavy cream
- ¼ teaspoon salt
- 2 tablespoons Demerara sugar
- 6 tablespoons water
- ½ teaspoon vanilla
- Chocolate shavings – to garnish

Directions:

1. Preheat oven to 300F.
2. Bring cream, salt and sugar to gentle simmer over medium heat, stirring until sugar dissolves.
3. Bring water and Demerara sugar to boil over medium-high heat, stirring until sugar dissolves. Continue to cook until browned and bubbly, stirring occasionally.
4. Remove from heat and stir in heavy cream mixture, until combined.
5. Whisk together yolks and vanilla and stir in cream mixture; pour custard into six jars.
6. Transfer jars into baking dish, filled with warm water; bake the crème for 40 minutes.
7. Cool to room temperature and garnish with chocolate shavings before serving.

Nutrition Facts

Serving Size 76 g

Amount Per Serving

Calories 200	Calories from Fat 127
	% Daily Value*
Total Fat 14.1g	22%
Saturated Fat 8.0g	40%
Trans Fat 0.0g	
Cholesterol 181mg	60%
Sodium 114mg	5%
Potassium 36mg	1%
Total Carbohydrates 17.3g	6%
Sugars 16.1g	
Protein 2.4g	
Vitamin A 12% •	Vitamin C 0%
Calcium 3% •	Iron 2%

Nutrition Grade D-

* Based on a 2000 calorie diet

Peanut butter pie

Serves: 12

Time: 20 minutes + inactive time

Ingredients:

- 8oz. wafer cookies, crumbled
- 8oz. mascarpone cheese
- 4oz. dark chocolate, chopped and melted (in microwave)
- 4oz. butter, melted
- ¼ cup peanuts, chopped
- ¾ cup powdered sugar
- 1 cup heavy cream, whipped to soft peaks
- 1 cup peanut butter

Directions:

1. Combine wafer crumbled cookies with melted butter in a jar.
2. Spoon three tablespoons into 12 4oz. Mason jars, pressing the mixture down with clean wine cork.
3. Spoon 1 tablespoon of melted chocolate over prepare crust, top with chopped peanuts refrigerate until chocolate is firm.
4. Meanwhile, combine mascarpone and peanut butter in a bowl; gradually stir in powdered sugar.
5. Stir in half of the whipped cream and when smooth, stir in remaining cream.
6. Pipe the mixture over prepare cookie crust and chill for 30 minutes; serve after.

Nutrition Facts

Serving Size 99 g

Amount Per Serving

Calories 455	Calories from Fat 314
	% Daily Value*
Total Fat 34.9g	54%
Saturated Fat 14.3g	71%
Trans Fat 0.0g	
Cholesterol 46mg	15%
Sodium 211mg	9%
Potassium 226mg	6%
Total Carbohydrates 31.3g	10%
Dietary Fiber 1.9g	7%
Sugars 14.4g	
Protein 9.3g	

Vitamin A 10%	•	Vitamin C 0%
Calcium 7%	•	Iron 15%

Nutrition Grade C

* Based on a 2000 calorie diet